1·2·3 Draw

Horses

A step-by-step guide

by
Freddie Levin

Peel Productions, Inc

Before you begin...

You will need:

- a pencil
- an eraser
- a pencil sharpener
- a ruler
- lots of paper (recycle and re-use)
- colored pencils for finished drawings
- a folder for saving your work
- a good light
- a comfortable place to draw

Now, let's begin!

Library of Congress Cataloging-in-Publication Data

Levin, Freddie.
 1-2-3 draw horses : a step-by-step guide / by Freddie Levin.
   p. cm.
 Includes index.
  ISBN 0-939217-61-9 (sewn paper : alk. paper)
1. Horses in art--Juvenile literature. 2. Colored pencil drawing--
Technique--Juvenile literature. I. Title: Horses. II. Title: One-two-three
draw horses. III. Title.

NC783.8.H65L48 2004
743.6'96655--dc22
                    2004015199

Distributed to the trade and art
markets in North America by

NORTH LIGHT BOOKS,
an imprint of F&W Publications, Inc.
4700 East Galbraith Road
Cincinnati, OH 45236

(800) 289-0963

Contents

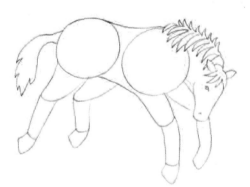

Important Drawing Tips:

1 Draw lightly at first (SKETCH!), so you can erase extra lines later.

2 The first few shapes are important. Notice the placement, sizes and positions of the first shapes.

3 Practice, practice, practice!

4 Have fun drawing horses!

Basic shapes

The drawings in this book begin with three basic shapes. Learn these shapes and practice drawing them.

Circle   Oval   Egg

Note to parents and teachers:

Just like swimming, riding a bike or playing the piano, drawing gets better and better with practice. Encourage children to practice the basic shapes of circles, eggs and ovals. For very young children or children with poor motor control, cut the shapes out of tag board and let them trace around them. The size, shape, and position of the first few shapes are important. Once the beginning shapes and their positions on the page are established, the rest of the drawing can be built around it.

To learn more about horses, check out the books at your public or school library.

Horse Vocabulary and Colors

To help us draw, let's learn some of the parts of a horse's body:

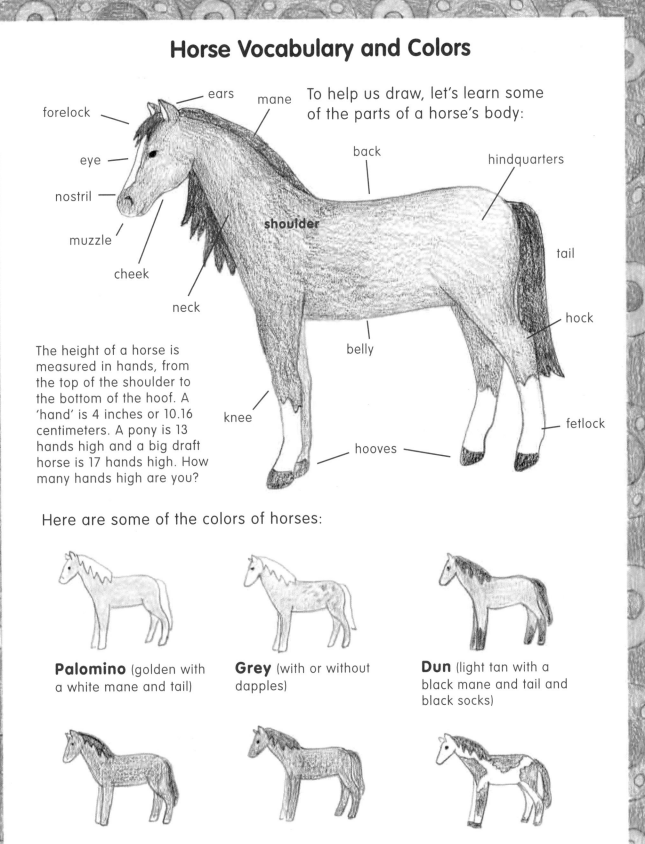

forelock
ears
mane
eye
nostril
muzzle
cheek
neck
back
shoulder
hindquarters
tail
hock
belly
fetlock
knee
hooves

The height of a horse is measured in hands, from the top of the shoulder to the bottom of the hoof. A 'hand' is 4 inches or 10.16 centimeters. A pony is 13 hands high and a big draft horse is 17 hands high. How many hands high are you?

Here are some of the colors of horses:

Palomino (golden with a white mane and tail)

Grey (with or without dapples)

Dun (light tan with a black mane and tail and black socks)

Bay (brown with a black mane and tail)

Chestnut (medium brown)

Piebald (large patches of black and white)

Prehistoric horse

Before there were horses, there was little Eohippus (the name means 'dawn horse'). Now extinct, it was the size of a fox and had toes instead of hooves. Gradually, over millions of years, as the environment changed, these little animals evolved into the horses we know today.

1 Sketch an oval for the body. Sketch a large and small circle for the head.

2 Draw two lines to connect the head circles. Draw two curving lines for the neck. Draw two ears.

3 Draw lines to begin the tail. Draw curved lines to begin two legs.

4 Draw an eye and a nostril. Add two more legs. Draw the tail tip.

5 Add feet with toes on each leg.

6 LOOK at the final drawing. Erase extra lines. Shade and color it. (Do we know if Eohippus had spots or stripes? No, we're just guessing!)

Excellent Eohippus!

Foal

A foal is a baby horse. A male foal is called a colt and a female is a filly. A foal can be up and running on its long legs within an hour of its birth. Most horses are born in the spring.

1 Lightly sketch an oval and a circle for the head, and an oval and a circle for the body. Notice the position of each shape.

2 Draw two lines to connect the head shapes. Add two curving neck lines. Draw a line for the back and one for the belly. Draw curved lines to begin two legs.

3 Draw two ears. Add an eye, a nose and a mouth. Draw a mane and a forelock. Add a tail. Begin two more legs.

4 Add lines for the inner ears. Look carefully at the shape of the legs. Draw the lower part of each leg. Draw a line for the hooves.

5 LOOK at the final drawing. Erase extra lines and color. The stripe on the foal's face is called a 'blaze'. The white markings on its legs are called 'socks'.

Fantastic foal!

Falabella (a miniature horse)

Kept as outdoor pets, Falabellas are delicate. Too small to be ridden, they need a lot of care. From Argentina, this miniature horse never stands over eight and a half hands high (34 inches from the top of the shoulder to the bottom of the hoof). The smallest horse ever recorded was 'Little Pumpkin' who was only 14 inches high.

1 Sketch a circle and a smaller circle for the head. Draw two larger circles for the body. Notice the positions of each circle.

2 Add an ear, an eye, a nostril and a mouth. Draw two lines to connect the head circles. Add two curving neck lines. Draw a curved line for the back and a curved line for the belly.

3 Draw four curved lines to begin the legs.

4 Draw a mane and forelock with short curved strokes. Draw a tail. Complete the lower part of each leg and add hooves.

5 LOOK at the final drawing. Erase extra lines. Shade and color. To show how small the horse is, draw it next to a girl or boy.

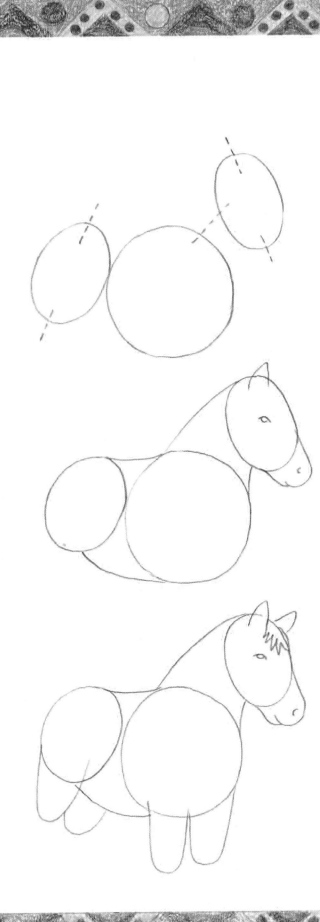

Draft horse

Powerful draft horses usually measure over sixteen hands high (54 inches). These gentle, calm horses are the biggest breed, and are still used in many parts of the world to pull heavy loads. During the Middle Ages, they carried knights with heavy armor into battle. Some famous breeds are Clydesdale (Scotland), Percheron (France) and Suffolk Punch (England).

1 Look carefully at the angle and positions of the head oval and the body circle and oval. Lightly sketch these.

2 Add the horse's muzzle. Draw an ear, an eye, a nostril, and a mouth. Draw two curving neck lines. Draw a curved line for the back and one for the belly.

3 Add another ear. Draw the forelock. Draw the beginning of four legs.

4 Draw a mane. Add a tail. Draw the lower part of each leg. Add hoofs.

5 LOOK at the final drawing. Draft horses often have shaggy hair around their hooves called 'feathering.' Erase extra lines. Shade and color. To show how big it is, draw your draft horse next to a man or a woman.

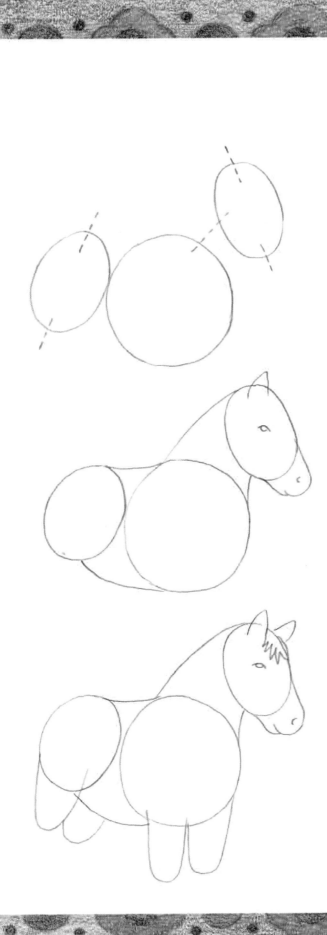

Shetland Pony

The tough, hardy Shetland Pony comes from the moors of Scotland. Smaller than horses (up to fourteen hands high), they are sure-footed and very strong for their size. They are popular as a children's riding horse.

1 Look carefully at the head and body shapes. Lightly sketch an oval and a circle for the body. Notice the angle of the head oval. Sketch it.

2 Draw an ear and an eye. Add the horse's muzzle. Draw a nostril and a mouth. Draw curving lines to complete the neck and body.

3 Add the forelock. Draw the beginning of four legs.

4 Erase extra sketch lines. Draw a tail. Add the pony's shaggy mane. Draw the lower part of the legs and the hooves. Draw the 'feathering' around the hooves.

5 LOOK at the final drawing. This pony has brown and white patches called 'skewbald.' Erase extra lines. Shade and color.

Pretty pony!

Mustang

Wild horses of the American West, Mustangs are descended from the horses brought by the Spanish explorers to the New World in the sixteenth century. Because of their speed and endurance, they were a favorite horse of Native American tribes.

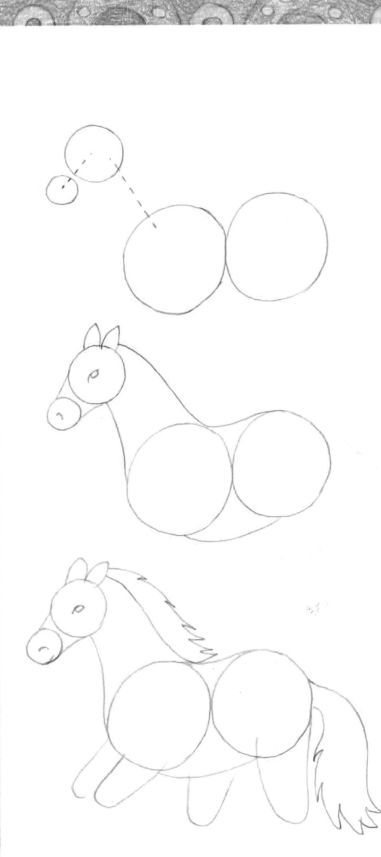

1 Look carefully at the angle and placement of each shape. Sketch a circle and a smaller circle for the head. Sketch two larger circles for the body.

2 Draw two lines to connect the head circles. Add two ears, an eye and a nostril. Draw two curving neck lines. Draw a curved line for the back and the belly.

3 Add a mouth. Draw a mane. Add a tail. Draw the beginning of four legs.

4 Draw the lower part of the legs and the hooves.

5 LOOK at the final drawing. Erase extra lines. Shade and color.

Are you remembering to sketch lightly at first?

Paso Fino

The Paso Fino is a gaited horse. That means it is born knowing fancy ways of walking. These small, beautiful horses from Puerto Rico are used mainly in horse shows and exhibitions to display riding skill.

1 LOOK at the distance between each shape. Notice the position and angle of each. Sketch an oval and a circle for the body. Sketch an oval and a small circle for the head.

2 Draw two lines to connect the head shapes. Draw two ears, an eye and a nostril. Draw two lines for its beautifully arched neck. Draw curved lines for the back and belly.

3 Draw a line inside each ear. Add a mane. Draw the beginning of two front legs and a back leg.

4 Add a forelock. Draw the distinctly curved tail. Notice the unusual way the horse holds up its legs. This is part of the Paso Fino's gait. Add the lower part of the back leg. Add a hoof. Draw the other back leg in the air. Add the lower part of the front legs and the hooves.

5 LOOK at the final drawing. Erase extra lines. Shade and color.

Bello caballo!

Palomino (pal- o-MEEN- o)

The Palomino is a color, not a breed. A showy golden coat with a white mane and tail makes it a favorite for movies. Let's draw this horse with a Western type saddle and a bridle. A Western saddle has a horn, or pommel, near the front. The pommel is used to anchor ropes during ranch work. A bridle is the set of straps around the horse's face that is connected to the reins. The bridle and the reins help the rider communicate with the horse.

1 LOOK at the angle and position of the circles. Notice the distance between them. Sketch a circle and a smaller circle for the head. Sketch two larger circles for the body.

2 Draw two lines to connect the head circles. Draw an ear, an eye, a nostril and a mouth. Add two curving neck lines. Draw a line for the back and one for the belly.

3 Draw a line for the inner ear and add another ear. Draw the mane. Draw the beginning of four legs.

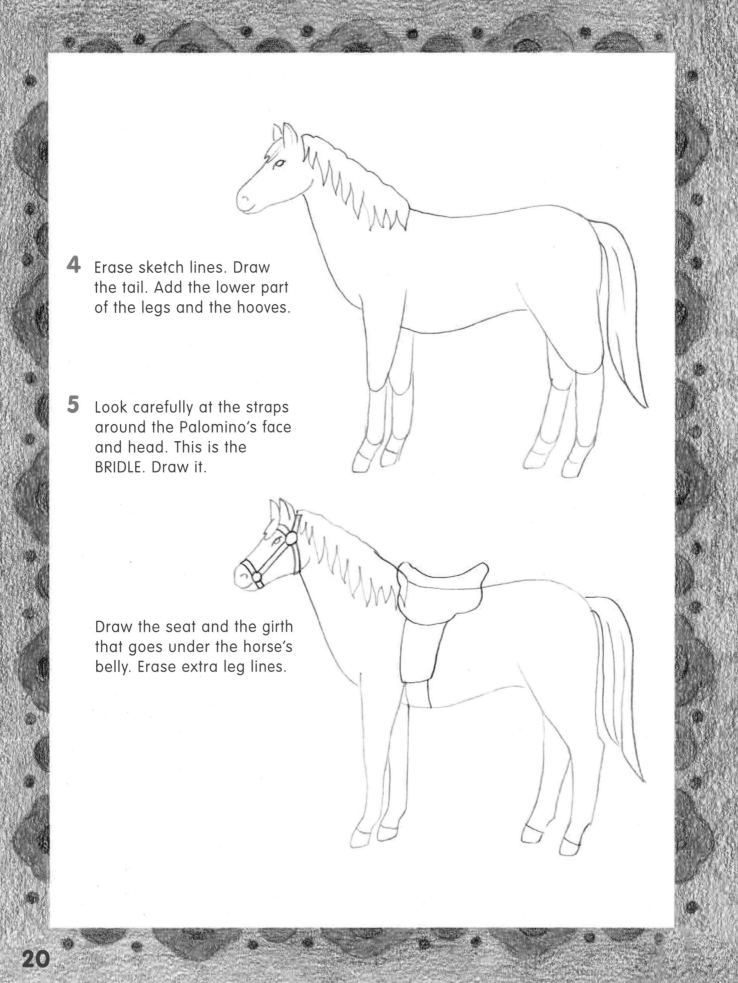

4 Erase sketch lines. Draw the tail. Add the lower part of the legs and the hooves.

5 Look carefully at the straps around the Palomino's face and head. This is the BRIDLE. Draw it.

Draw the seat and the girth that goes under the horse's belly. Erase extra leg lines.

6 Draw the horn or pommel at the front of the saddle. Add the reins. Draw the stirrup. Draw the blanket that goes under the saddle.

7 LOOK at the final drawing. Shade and color your Palomino. Add decorations to the saddle. Beautifully decorated Western saddles were originally made by the Spanish Gauchos.

Super Saddle!

Appaloosa

Horses were highly valued by the Plains Indians who used them for hunting and transportation. Appaloosas were developed by the Nez Perce Indians of the American Northwest. The Appaloosa is easily recognized by their spotted markings.

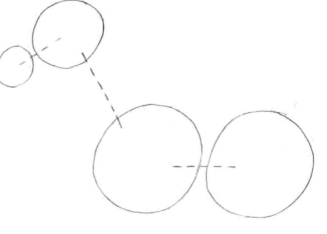

1 Look at the head circles and the body circles. See the distance between them. Sketch the head circles. Sketch two larger circles for the body.

2 Draw lines to connect the head circles. Add an ear, an eye, a nostril and a mouth. Draw two curving neck lines. Draw a line for the back and one for the belly.

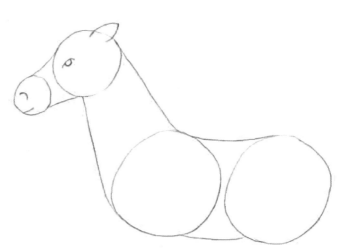

3 Add a forelock and a mane. Draw a line for the inner ear. Add another ear. Draw the tail. Sketch the curved lines to begin three legs.

4 Draw the lower part of the three legs. Add a second hind leg. Draw the hooves.

5 Look at the final drawing. Erase extra lines. Shade and color. Make the Appaloosa's spotted coat.

Awesome Appaloosa!

Rodeo horse (Quarter Horse)

(The next drawings are more
complicated because they are horses
plus riders. Let's start with the horse
and then, step by step, add the rider.
Don't forget to draw lightly so you
can erase extra lines.)

A rodeo is a contest where cowboys
and cowgirls can show off their
roping and riding skills. The favorite
breed for ranch work is the American
quarter horse, so named for the
speed it could run in a quarter of a
mile. Not only are quarter horses fast
but they can stop and turn on a dime.

1 Look carefully at the body
and head circles. Notice the
angle of the body. Measure
how far it is from the head.
Sketch two large circles for
the body. Look at the
position of the head. Sketch
a circle and a smaller circle
for the head.

2 Draw two lines connecting
the head circles. Draw two
ears, an eye and a nostril.
Draw two curving neck
lines. Draw a line for the
back and one for the belly.

3 Add the tail. Draw the
beginning of four legs.

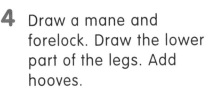

4 Draw a mane and forelock. Draw the lower part of the legs. Add hooves.

5 The horse is complete. Erase extra lines. Now we will draw the rider. Notice the angle of the head and body. Sketch an egg shape for the head. Measure how far the head is from the horse's back. Sketch a rectangle for the rider's upper body. Draw the first part of the rider's legs.

6 Draw one outstretched arm. Draw a bandanna around the rider's neck. Draw the lower part of the front leg. Draw the saddle seat.

7 Draw the brim of the rider's hat. Add ties to the bandanna. Draw two hands. Draw the boot. Add a stirrup around the boot.

8 Add the crown of the hat. Draw the rider's face. Draw the rider's braids. Draw a line down the center of the shirt. Draw the girth of the saddle around the horse's belly. Put a rope in the rider's left hand.

LOOK at the final drawing. Erase extra
lines. Shade and color.

Ride 'em, cowgirl!

Pony Express

In 1848, many Americans moved to California because of the Gold Rush. There was no transcontinental railroad yet and mail had to be put on ships that slowly sailed around the tip of South America. This took months. From 1860 to 1861, a faster way to deliver mail was invented. Letters were taken by Pony Express in a sort of relay race. Each rider would race his horse a certain distance then hand over the mail to the next rider until the mail reached California. It was very tiring for the horses and the riders and when the railroad was finally connected, the Pony Express was disbanded.

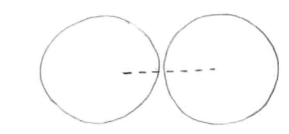

1 Sketch an oval for the head. Sketch two larger circles for the body.

2 Draw an ear and an eye. Draw the muzzle and nostril. Draw two curving neck lines. Draw a line for the back and one for the belly.

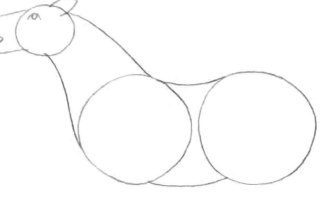

3 Draw an inner ear. The tail is stretched out because the horse is running fast. Draw the tail. Draw the beginnings of four legs.

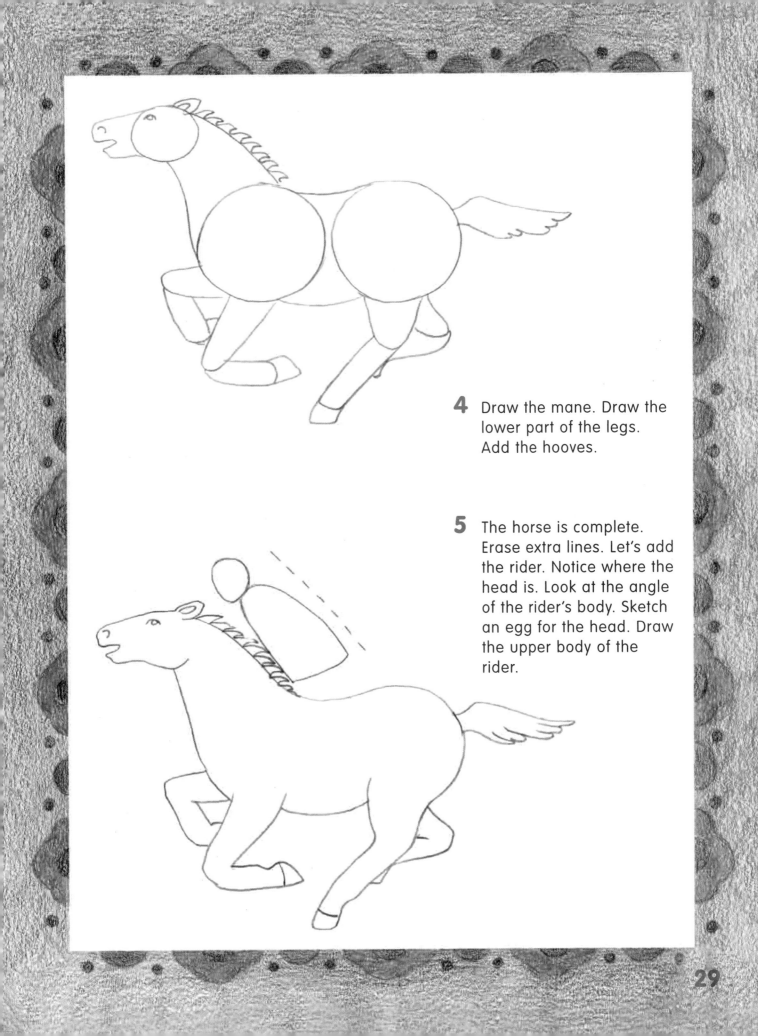

4 Draw the mane. Draw the lower part of the legs. Add the hooves.

5 The horse is complete. Erase extra lines. Let's add the rider. Notice where the head is. Look at the angle of the rider's body. Sketch an egg for the head. Draw the upper body of the rider.

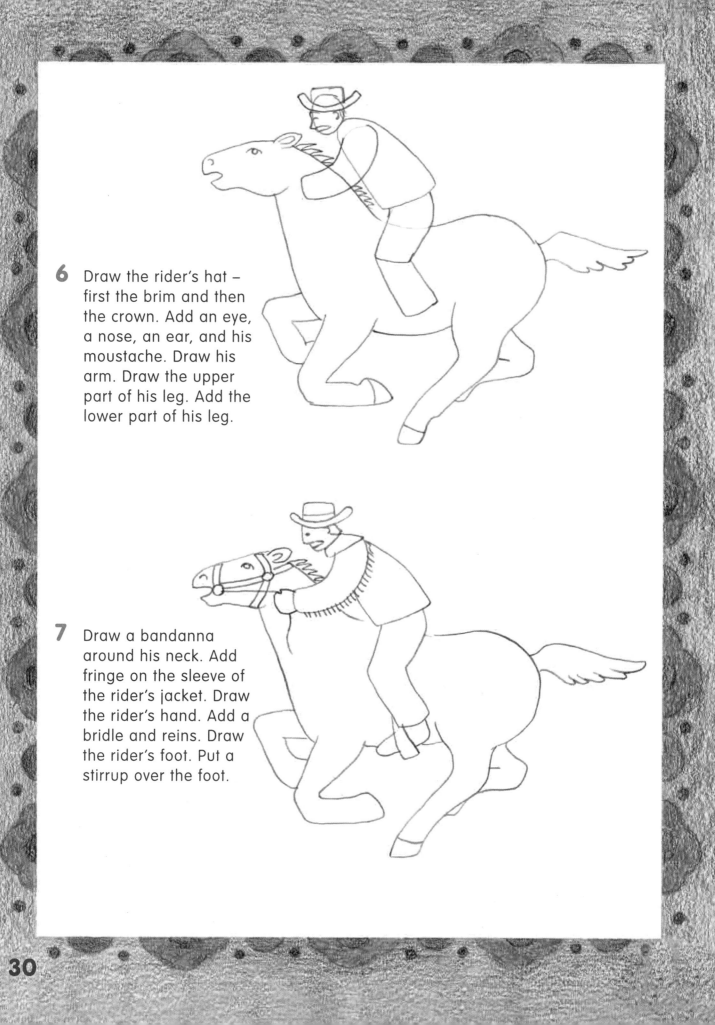

6   Draw the rider's hat –
first the brim and then
the crown. Add an eye,
a nose, an ear, and his
moustache. Draw his
arm. Draw the upper
part of his leg. Add the
lower part of his leg.

7   Draw a bandanna
around his neck. Add
fringe on the sleeve of
the rider's jacket. Draw
the rider's hand. Add a
bridle and reins. Draw
the rider's foot. Put a
stirrup over the foot.

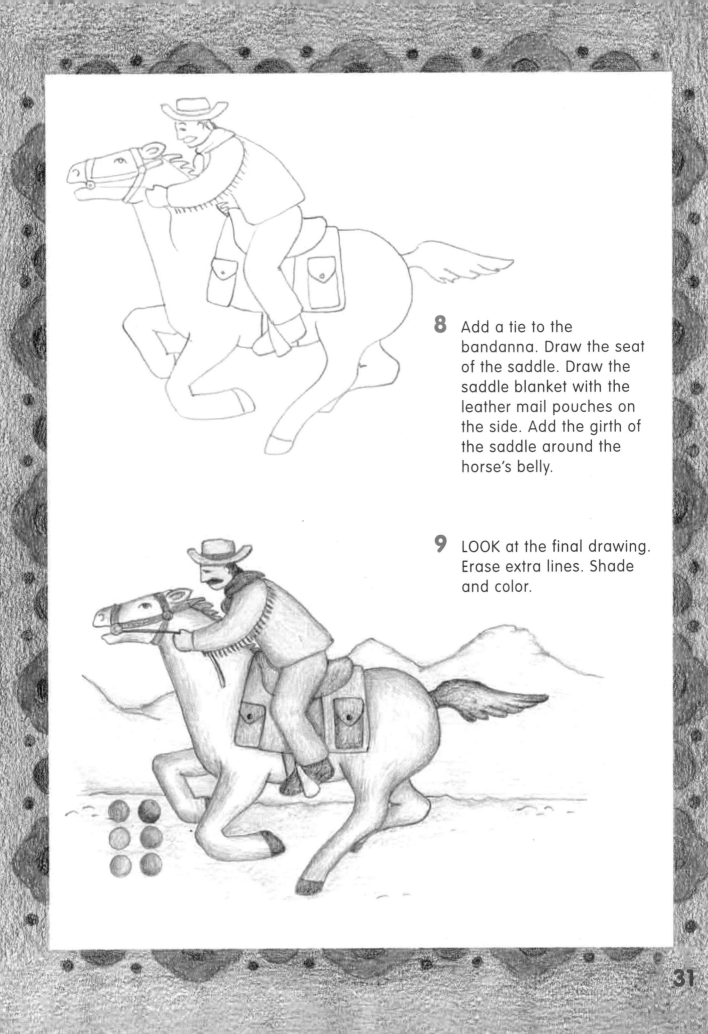

8 Add a tie to the bandanna. Draw the seat of the saddle. Draw the saddle blanket with the leather mail pouches on the side. Add the girth of the saddle around the horse's belly.

9 LOOK at the final drawing. Erase extra lines. Shade and color.

Circus Horse or Knabstrup (kuh-NOB-strup)

Knabstrups are originally from Denmark. This intelligent, easily trained horse, with its showy polka dot markings, make it a favorite for circuses.

1 Notice the angles of the head and body circles. Measure the distance between them. Sketch the two small circles for the head. Sketch two larger circles for the body.

2 Draw two lines to connect the head circles. Draw two curving neck lines. Draw a curved line for the back and one for the belly.

3 Draw two ears, an eye, a nostril and a mouth. Draw the beginning of two legs.

4 Erase sketch lines. Draw the mane. Draw the saddle seat and the girth around the horse's belly. Add the lower part of the legs.

5 Draw the bridle and reins. Draw two more legs. Add lines for the hooves.

6 Look at the final drawing. Add a tail. Decorate the saddle. Put some plumes on top of the horse's head. Draw the polka dot markings on your Knabstrup!

Sensational Circus Horse!

Dressage (dress- AHJ)

The word 'dressage' comes from a French word that means 'to train.' It is the training of a horse to a very high level. In a dressage competition, horses are judged on the precision of their movements. It is meant to show perfect harmony between horse and rider.

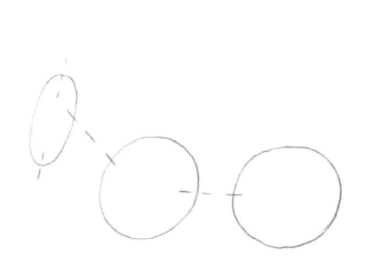

1 Notice the angle of the head. Sketch an oval for the head and two circles for the body.

2 Draw an ear, an eye, a nostril and a mouth. Draw a forelock. This horse's neck is very arched. Draw two curving neck lines. Draw a line for the back of the horse and one for the belly.

3 Draw the beginning of three legs. Add the tail.

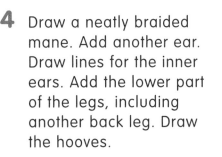

4 Draw a neatly braided mane. Add another ear. Draw lines for the inner ears. Add the lower part of the legs, including another back leg. Draw the hooves.

5 This horse is complete Let's add the rider. Notice how straight the rider is sitting. Measure how high above the horse's back the head and upper body are. Sketch an egg for the head. Draw the upper body.

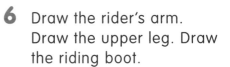

6 Draw the rider's arm. Draw the upper leg. Draw the riding boot.

7 Draw the rider's special hat. Add the nose, eye, and ear. Draw a hand. Draw a bridle on the horse and a rein. Add the tail of the special riding jacket.

8 Look how straight she is sitting. Make the rider's hair pulled back in a neat bun. Add some buttons to the rider's sleeve. Draw the saddle. Add the girth that goes around the horse's belly. Draw the stirrup over the boot.

9 LOOK at the final drawing. Erase extra lines. Shade and color.

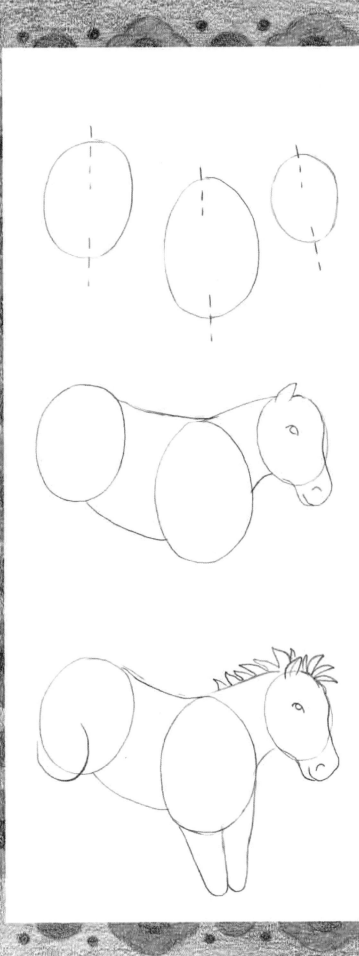

Show Jumping (Arabian)

In a show jumping event, the horse and rider team is judged for speed and accuracy in clearing the barriers. Bred in the deserts of the Middle East by Bedouin tribes, the Arabians were known for speed and endurance. Highly spirited, with a fine head and an arched neck, they are considered by some to be the most beautiful horses in the world.

1 Look at the angle of the ovals. See where they are in relation to each other. Sketch the three ovals.

2 Notice that an Arabian's profile is slightly curved from forehead to the muzzle. Add the horse's muzzle. Draw an ear, an eye, a nostril and a mouth. Add two curved neck lines. Draw a line for the horse's back and one for the horse's belly.

3 Add a line for the inner ear. Draw the mane and forelock. Draw the beginning of the back leg. Draw the beginning of two front legs.

4 Notice that the two back legs are shaped like a letter 'J.' Draw the back legs. Draw the lower part of the front legs. Add hooves. Draw a tail.

5 The horse is complete. Erase extra lines on the horse. Now let's draw the rider. Notice the angle of the head and upper body. Measure the distance between the horse and the rider. Sketch an egg for the head. Draw the upper body of the rider.

6 Draw a cap on the rider. This is a hard hat that protects the rider's head. Draw two arms.

7 Add a center line to the rider's jacket. Draw the flap of the jacket. Draw a hand. Draw a bridle and reins on the horse. Draw the beginning of the rider's leg.

8 Add a hat line. Draw the chin strap of the hat. Draw eyes, a nose, and a mouth on the rider's face. Draw the rider's hair pulled back neatly in a bun. Add the lower part of the rider's leg. Draw the saddle seat and the girth that goes around the belly of the horse. Draw the boot. Add a stirrup over the foot of the rider.

9 LOOK at the final drawing. Erase extra lines. Shade and color. Give your horse and rider a fence to jump over. Did your horse win? Draw a blue ribbon for Best in Show! *(See page 64.)*

Lippizaner (lip-pet-ZAHN-er)

Lippizaners are the showy white horses of the Spanish Riding School in Vienna, Austria. The School was founded in the 1500's. The horses and riders are trained, over many months to perform complicated, precise steps, leaping and posing in movements that are like a 'horse ballet.'

1 Notice the arrangement of all four shapes. Look at the angle of the circles. Sketch a circle and a smaller circle for the head. Sketch two larger circles for the body.

2 Draw two lines to connect the head circles. Draw ears, an eye, a nostril and a mouth. Draw two curving neck lines. Draw a line for the back of the horse and one for the belly.

3 Draw the inner ear. Draw the beginning of four legs. Add a tail.

43

4 Draw a mane. Add lines in the tail. Complete the lower part of the legs. Draw the hooves.

5 The horse is complete. Erase extra lines. Now let's draw the rider. Look at how far the rider is above the horse. Notice the angle of the rider's body. Sketch an oval for the head. Draw the upper body shape. Draw two neck lines.

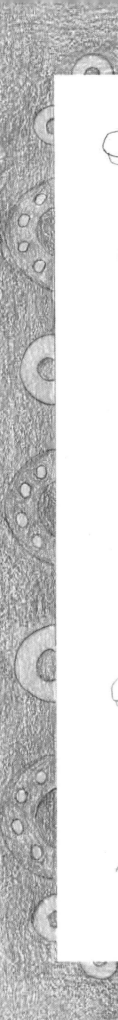

6 Draw the rider's hat. Draw the arm and a hand. Draw the long coat tail.

7 Draw a face on the rider. Draw the rider's upper leg. Add the boot. Draw a bridle on the horse's head. Add a rein.

8 Draw a collar and buttons on the rider's coat. Draw a saddle. Draw the girth that goes around the belly of the horse. Add a stirrup over the rider's boot.

9 To finish your drawing, erase extra lines, shade and color.

Leapin' Lippizaner!

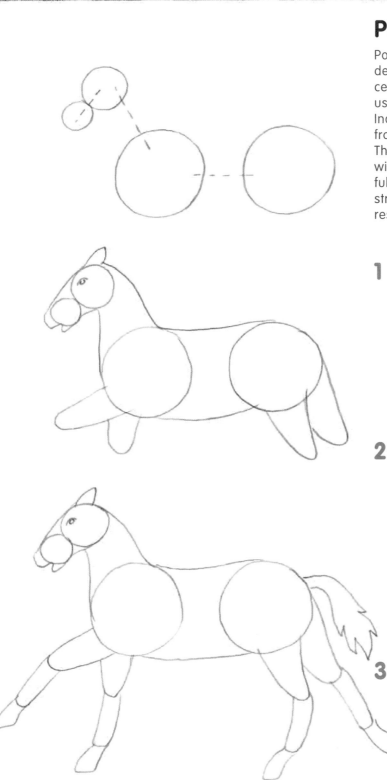

Polo pony

Polo is a very old game. It was developed in India in the seventh century. The original breed of horse used for polo was the Manipuri of India. Now, most polo ponies are from Argentina. Polo is a fast game. The rider must hit a ball to a goal with a mallet while his horse is at full gallop. A polo pony must be strong, fast, agile, and trained to respond instantly to the rider.

1 Notice the angles of the circles. Measure how far the head is from the body. Sketch a circle and a smaller circle for the head. Sketch two larger circles for the body.

2 Draw lines to connect the head circles. Draw the horse's muzzle. Draw an eye and an ear. Draw two curving neck lines. Draw a line for the back and one for the belly. Begin four legs.

3 Complete the lower part of each leg. Draw the hooves. Add a tail.

4 The horse is complete. Notice how far above the horse the rider will be. Look at the angle of the rider's body. Sketch an oval for the head and a rectangle for the upper body.

5 Draw the brim of the rider's cap. Add neck lines. Draw two arms. Add hands. Draw the beginning of the rider's leg.

6 Draw the rest of the cap. Add eyes, nose and a mouth. Draw the lower part of the rider's leg and the boot. Draw the upper part of the rider's second leg.

7 Draw lines for the rider's polo shirt. Add fingers to the right hand. Draw the saddle. Add a knee pad to the rider's leg. Draw a stirrup over the boot. Draw the girth of the saddle around the horse's belly.

8 Draw a bridle and reins on the horse. Give the rider a polo mallet. Put a number on the sleeve of the polo shirt. Add protective tape to the horse's lower legs.

9 LOOK at the final drawing. Erase extra lines. Shade and color.

Race Horse (Thoroughbred)

Horse racing is one of the oldest sports in the world. The earliest known race track dates back to the Roman Empire. It is a fast and furious sport and can be quite dangerous. The breed of horse most commonly used in horse racing is the Thoroughbred. Thoroughbreds are originally from England and are bred for speed.

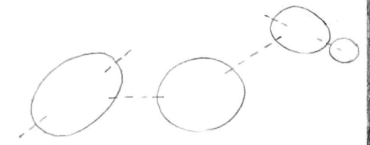

1 Look at the angles of all the shapes. Measure the distance between them. Sketch an oval and a small circle for the head. Sketch a circle and an oval for the body.

2 Draw lines to connect the head oval and circle. Add an ear, an eye, a nostril and a mouth. Draw two curving neck lines. Draw a line for the back and one for the belly.

3 Draw a tail. Draw the beginnings of four legs.

4 Add a mane. Draw the lower part of four legs. Add the hooves.

5 The horse is complete. Now we will start the rider, who is called a jockey. Notice the angle of the two shapes. Sketch an oval for the jockey's head. Draw the jockey's chest.

7 Draw the jockey's cap. Add an arm. Draw the upper part of the jockey's leg.

8 Add the jockey's hand. Draw a bridle and reins on the horse. Draw the lower part of the jockey's leg and the boot.

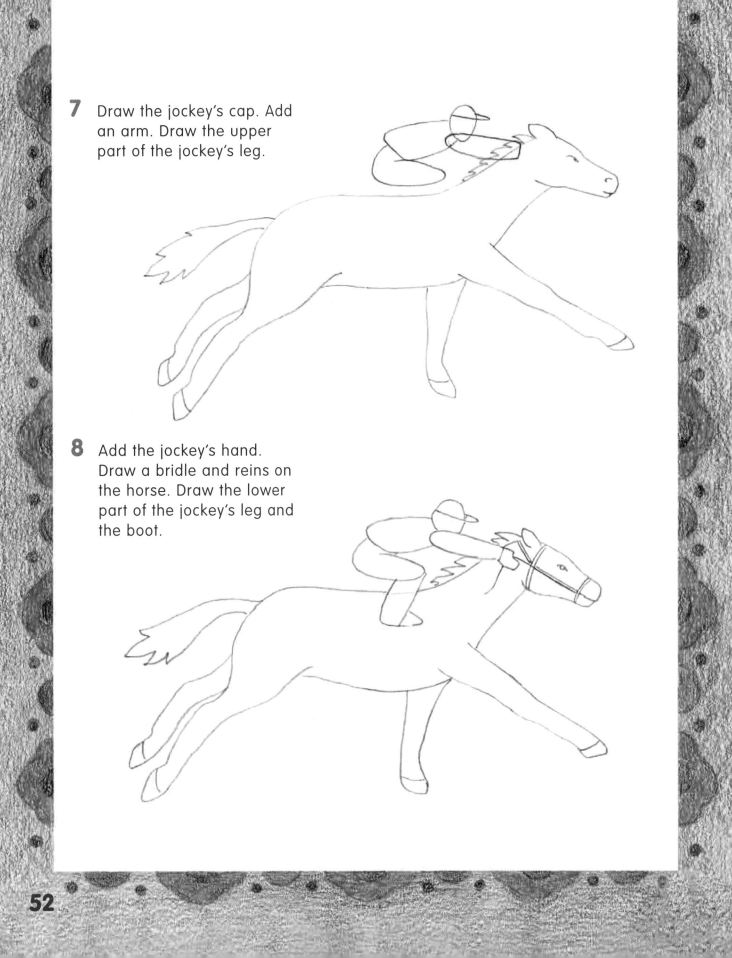

9 Add an eye, a nose and an ear to the jockey's face. Put dots on the shirt. Draw a saddle on the horse. Draw a stirrup on the jockey's boot. Put the girth around the horse's belly. Give the horse a number.

10 LOOK at the final drawing. Shade and color.

Some famous race horses were Man O' War, SeaBiscuit, War Admiral, and Secretariat. What would you name your race horse?

Police horse (Morgan)

Police horses and their mounted officers are used to patrol parks and manage traffic in city streets. The height of the horse gives the officer a high viewpoint which is an advantage in crowd control. Morgans are strong, intelligent and have wonderful temperaments. They are one of America's most popular breeds. All Morgans can be traced back to one horse owned by Justin Morgan, an eighteenth century Massachusetts schoolteacher.

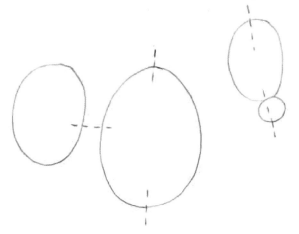

1 Look at the body and the head shapes. Measure the distance between these. Sketch an oval and a small circle for the head. Sketch a large egg and an oval for the body.

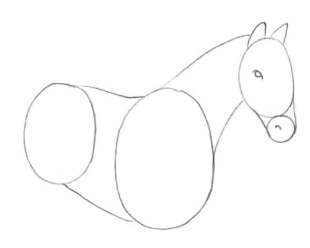

2 Draw two lines to connect the head shapes. Draw two ears, an eye and a nostril. Draw two curving neck lines. Draw a line for the back and one for the belly.

3 Draw the inner ear. Draw the beginning of four legs.

4 Draw the forelock, mane, and tail. Add a mouth line. Draw the lower part of the legs. Draw the hooves.

5 The police horse is complete. Erase extra lines. Now let's start the rider. Look at the angle of the shapes. Measure how far they are above the horse's back. Sketch an egg for the head and a rectangle for the upper body.

6 Draw the helmet. Draw the short sleeve shirt lines, slanting down from the head. Draw two arms. Add the right hand.

7 Put a badge on the cap. Draw an ear, an eye, a nose, and a mouth on the police officer's face. Draw her hair under her cap. Draw a curved line, under her right arm, to begin the leg. Add the lower leg and a boot. Draw a bridle and reins on the horse.

8 Add a collar, badges, and a belt to the officer's uniform. Draw the saddle. Draw a stirrup over the boot.

8 LOOK at the final drawing. Add details. Shade and color. Draw a city scape for your police horse and police officer.

Donkey

A donkey is a horse's little cousin. Donkeys have been helping people since 4000 BC in Egypt and Africa. They have the strength and stamina to carry heavy loads over long distances in harsh terrain. A male donkey is a jack and a female donkey is a jennie.

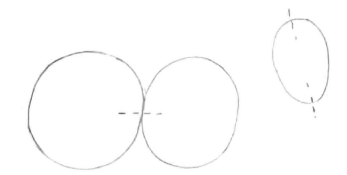

1 Look at the position of each shape. Notice the angle of the head shape. Measure how far it is from the body. Sketch a large circle and a slightly smaller circle for the body. Sketch an egg for the head.

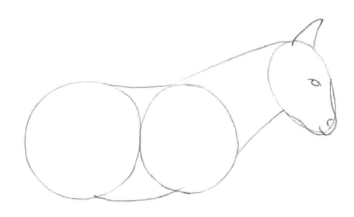

2 Draw the donkey's muzzle. Add an eye, an ear, a nostril and a mouth. Draw two curving neck lines. Draw a line for the back and one for the belly.

3 Add a tail. Draw the beginning of four legs.

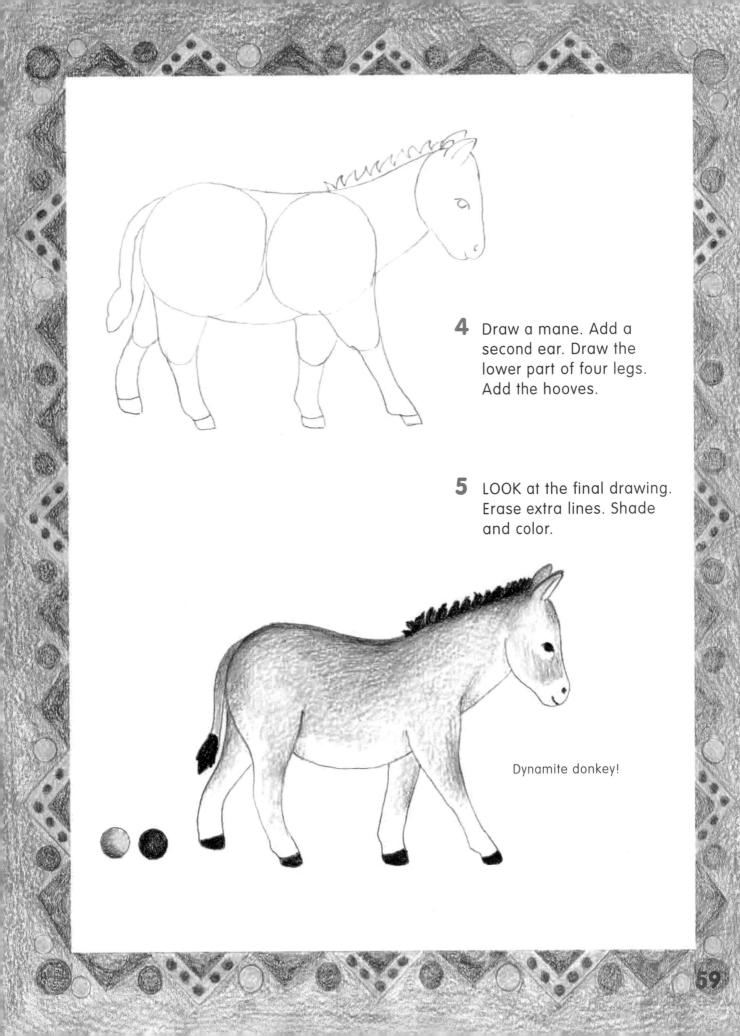

4 Draw a mane. Add a second ear. Draw the lower part of four legs. Add the hooves.

5 LOOK at the final drawing. Erase extra lines. Shade and color.

Dynamite donkey!

Przewalski's horse (per – juh- WALL- ski)

Przewalski's horse is the only known breed of truly wild horse. It was discovered in western Mongolia by a Russian colonel in 1881. It is extinct in the wild and today only exists in zoos. It is the link between earlier breeds of horses and the modern horse of today. Przewalski's horse looks like the horses in a cave painting.

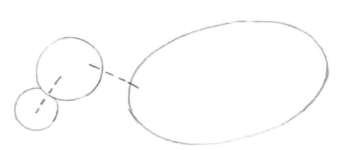

1 Notice the angle and position of each shape. Look at the distance between the head and the body shapes. Sketch a circle and a smaller circle for the head. Sketch a large oval for the body.

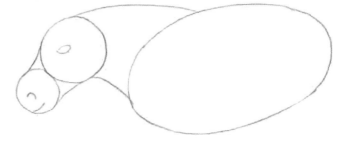

2 Draw lines to connect the head circles. Add an eye, a nostril, and a mouth. Draw two curving neck lines.

3 Draw two ears. Complete the eye. Draw the beginning of four legs.

4 Add a shaggy mane and forelock. Draw a tail. Draw the lower part of four legs. Add the hooves.

5 LOOK at the final drawing. Erase extra lines. Shade and color.

Zebra

Zebras are a horse's wild cousins. Famous for their spectacular black and white striped markings, they live in herds in African grasslands.

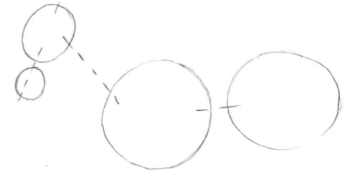

1 Notice the placement and angle of the head and body shapes. Sketch a circle and a smaller circle for the head. Sketch two larger circles for the body.

2 Draw two ears. Add two lines to connect the head circles. Draw two curving neck lines. Draw a line for the back and one for the belly. Draw the beginning of four legs.

3 Add an eye, a nostril, and a mouth. The mane stands up straight and bristly. Draw it. Add the tail. Like a donkey tail, it has a tuft of hair at the end.

4 Draw the lower part of four legs. Add the hooves.

5 LOOK at the final drawing. Erase extra lines. Draw the zebra's spectacular black stripes.

Index

Learn about other
drawing books online at
www.drawbooks.com